COMPETITIVE STRATEGY
Planning Your Organization's Success

Sarah M. Layton, Ph.D.
Alfred B. Hurd, MBA
William G. Lipsey, MBA

A FIFTY-MINUTE™ SERIES BOOK

CRISP PUBLICATIONS, INC.
Menlo Park, California

COMPETITIVE STRATEGY
Planning Your Organization's Success

Sarah M. Layton, Ph.D.
Alfred B. Hurd, MBA
William G. Lipsey, MBA

CREDITS
Managing Editor: **Kathleen Barcos**
Editor: **Janis Paris**
Typesetting: **ExecuStaff**
Cover Design: **Carol Harris**
Artwork: **Ralph Mapson**

Copyright © 1995 by Crisp Publications, Inc.

Printed in the United States of America by Bawden Printing Company.

English language Crisp books are distributed worldwide. Our major international distributors include:

CANADA: Reid Publishing Ltd., Box 69559–109 Thomas St., Oakville, Ontario, Canada L6J 7R4. TEL: (905) 842-4428, FAX: (905) 842-9327

Raincoast Books Distribution Ltd., 112 East 3rd Avenue, Vancouver, British Columbia, Canada V5T 1C8. TEL: (604) 873-6581, FAX: (604) 874-2711

AUSTRALIA: Career Builders, P.O. Box 1051, Springwood, Brisbane, Queensland, Australia 4127. TEL: 841-1061, FAX: 841-1580

NEW ZEALAND: Career Builders, P.O. Box 571, Manurewa, Auckland, New Zealand. TEL: 266-5276, FAX: 266-4152

JAPAN: Phoenix Associates Co., Mizuho Bldg. 2-12-2, Kami Osaki, Shinagawa-Ku, Tokyo 141, Japan. TEL: 3-443-7231, FAX: 3-443-7640

Selected Crisp titles are also available in other languages. Contact International Rights Manager Suzanne Kelly at (415) 323-6100 for more information.

Library of Congress Catalog Card Number 95-67038
Layton, Sarah M., Alfred B. Hurd and William G. Lipsey
Competitive Strategy
ISBN 1-56052-350-6

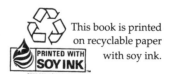

This book is printed on recyclable paper with soy ink.

PRINTED WITH **SOY INK**

ABOUT THIS BOOK

Competitive Strategy is not like most books. It has a unique self-paced format that encourages a reader to become personally involved. Designed to be "read with a pencil," there are exercises, activities, assessments and cases that invite participation.

This book focuses on competitive strategy planning, a team-based process that helps organizations build a competitive advantage in the marketplace by developing and implementing strategies that grow the business.

Competitive Strategy can be used effectively in a number of ways. Here are some possibilities:

► **Individual Study.** Because the book is self-instructional, all that is needed is a quiet place, some time and a pencil. Completing the activities and exercises will provide valuable feedback, as well as practical ideas for improving your business successes and profitability.

► **Workshops and Seminars.** This book is ideal for use during, or as pre-assigned reading prior to, a workshop or seminar. With the basics in hand, the quality of participation will improve. More time can be spent practicing concept extensions and applications during the program.

► **College Programs.** Thanks to the format, brevity and low cost, this book is ideal for short courses and extension programs.

There are other possibilities that depend on the objectives of the user. One thing is certain: even after it has been read, this book will serve as excellent reference material that can be easily reviewed.

ABOUT THE AUTHORS

Sarah M. Layton, Ph.D.

A seasoned veteran of the sales and marketing industry, Sarah Layton has been involved in business strategy for over a decade. Her in-depth experience includes over 10 years with Fortune 500 companies and formal research in the areas of Strategic Quality Planning and Competitive Marketing Strategies. Dr. Layton is president of her own multimillion dollar company, Mishalanie, Layton and Associates. She also serves as Corporate Strategist with the Hamilton Strategic Management Group.

A prolific writer, Dr. Layton introduced her book *Marketing Strategies, the SMART Formula* at an international congress in Chicago and most recently contributed to *Association Management*, *Modern Healthcare*, *Private Clubs*, *Club Management*, *Physician*, and *Source*.

The organizations that have benefited from her concepts include Siemens, Voluntary Hospitals of America, GE Capital, MCI, CNN, Toshiba, Dun and Bradstreet, and The American Management Association. Dr. Layton has also recently received the President's Award for Distinguished Service from the National Speakers Association.

Alfred B. Hurd, MBA

Alfred B. Hurd, Senior Consultant and Planning Director for the Hamilton Strategic Management Group, has worked for more than 30 years with companies of all sizes solving problems by designing and implementing practical, creative solutions using his background in: strategic planning, management practice, computer systems, communications, mechanics, human behavior, and training.

He has helped frame strategic plans for companies in pharmaceuticals, food, insurance, service, and manufacturing. He has trained hundreds of project managers at universities and in businesses of all kinds: financial, information systems, process, heavy equipment, and utilities.

He has published articles in *Computerworld* and the *Journal of Systems Management*. Currently he is extending his problem-solving trainer's kit: *What Changed?*; *Problem Solving* with a *Casebook of Team Problems*.

Mr. Hurd graduated from Harvard College with an A.B. in English (honors) and from the Harvard Business School with an M.B.A. in Control Systems and Organizational Behavior.

William G. Lipsey, MBA

William G. Lipsey is President of the Hamilton Strategic Management Group, Inc., a company that provides strategic management services to a broad range of clients in both the public and private sector. Mr. Lipsey works with a selected number of Hamilton Group clients representing a broad range of industries, including traditional manufacturing, distribution, and retailing. In addition, he has extensive experience in the financial services sector, specifically banking and insurance.

Prior to joining the planning group of the American Management Association (the predecessor organization to the Hamilton Group) over 10 years ago, Mr. Lipsey had an extensive career with the Exxon Corporation spanning more than 20 years. He focused on International Business and spent many years with operating and management organizations in the Far East, Australia and Europe.

His educational background includes a B.A. degree in Political Science from Colgate University and an M.B.A. from the Harvard Business School.

The Hamilton Strategic Management Group

The Hamilton Strategic Management Group is working with organizations and individuals to assist them in forming plans that lead to competitive advantage in the marketplace. The group's strategic management experts act as change agents, advisors, and instructors as their clients develop and implement programs and processes appropriate to the unique characteristics and needs of each organization.

This book is based on the well-tested and systematic logic underlying the Hamilton Group Planning Process, a process which is available to clients throughout North America.

ABOUT THE AUTHORS (continued)

For more information on Hamilton Group facilitated processes and training programs, please call:

Hamilton Strategic Management Group
P.O. Box 627, Hamilton, NY 13346
(800) 882-2740   (407) 877-2238

The Hamilton Group is the independent exclusive licensee of the American Management Association for AMA Planning Services.

Acknowledgments

Thanks to Bruce Harpster for his thoughtful editing and support.

CONTENTS

INTRODUCTION

Competitive Strategy presents a well-tested process for bringing the future into the present so a management team can act *now* to shape the future. That team may come from any organization: businesses, not-for-profit organizations, volunteer groups, churches, even families. Whenever people are gathered for mutual benefit, they can profit from planning their competitive strategy.

Although one new initiative after another (such as Total Quality Management (TQM), Right Sizing, Down Sizing, Empowerment, and the like) has swept through corporate America, strategic planning for competitive advantage remains fundamental to all these management tools. A survey of over 200 executives in North America reported in *Management Review*[1] found that 42 percent had adopted eleven or more initiatives within the preceding five years and 60 percent reported three or more initiatives in the last year and a half. Although two-thirds reported short-term gains, a full two out of three admitted that their internal structures and employee morale were "worse" or "the same"! All of these initiatives can be valuable when they are applied to achieve the vision of an organization's competitive strategy—but these tools are seldom ends in themselves.

This book uses business examples to illustrate the Competitive Strategy Process, but the reader can easily translate business titles and areas of interest to their own organization; for example, "Chief Financial Officer" can be understood as "Treasurer," and "Gross Revenue" as "Grants" or "Contributions."

Readers who want to develop a competitive strategy for their own organizations can use this book as their guide. The book describes the process of developing a competitive strategy; readers use their experience with their own particular business to generate the insights and creativity needed to understand issues, solve problems, and set new directions. The team that follows the process presented in this book—working through all its parts and thoughtfully completing all exercises—will produce a rewarding competitive strategy. In addition, they will find themselves more than ever united as an effective team, and they will have learned much about how to manage the projects and the managers that will implement the plan. After all, research shows that organizations with a sound competitive strategy and effective implementation have a bottom-line growth of 10 percent per year compared with only 1 percent for organizations without such a strategy.[2]

---

1. *Management Review*, The American Management Association, October 1994.
2. Based on research conducted in 1991 by Mishalanie, Layton & Associates, Inc.

PLANNING

The Key to Competitive Strategy

STARTING OUT

Competitive Strategy answers the question: "How do we get where we want to go with what we have or can get?" Successful answers are based on a great deal of straightforward hard work illuminated by creativity at critical points. It is easy to understand but difficult to do. It is "difficult" because creating an effective competitive strategy requires senior managers to take time from their daily routine and think strategically and hard about their business, their competition, the marketplace and the environment. This kind of thinking and the data gathering it requires is often unfamiliar, but senior managers are responsible for strategy. This book tells them how to do the work that leads to competitive success.

The core process in developing a competitive strategy for your organization or for yourself is planning. Generally speaking, Competitive Strategy Planning concentrates on new directions and growth more than on cost savings and efficiencies of operation. It concentrates on "top line" rather than "bottom line" improvement. Both elements are addressed, of course, but the outward-looking view of competitive strategy toward customers and markets takes precedence.

It is also important to understand what the process is *not.* It is not a long-term financial projection, nor is it individual managers filling out a preordained set of forms. It is not next year's budget or "operating plan." Rather, Competitive Strategy Planning is a team-based process that focuses on building competitive advantage in the marketplace by developing and implementing strategies that build the business. It absolutely requires the involvement of senior management for its development and the whole organization's commitment to its implementation. Without these, any plan is a worthless document no matter how handsomely produced and bound.

Simple stated, the process of developing a competitive strategy asks and answers three questions:

- Where are we?

- Where do we want to be?

- How can we get there?

Once the competitive strategy is clear, implementation can follow—secure in the knowledge that the chosen tasks are the best and wisest for the organization.

STARTING OUT (continued)

A Six-Part Process

The process of developing a competitive strategy has six parts, each of which differs sharply from the others. Every one is vital and the six must be done strictly in sequence. The diagram *Competitive Strategy Development Process* illustrates these steps, and the chapters that follow discuss them in detail:

1. Preplanning

Selecting and training the team and organizing for planning

2. Intelligence Gathering

Collecting data about products, markets, government regulations, and technology, as well as about competitors, customers, and employees for every aspect of your business

3. Analysis

Thinking about what the data mean and using this meaning to illuminate management's understanding of the business

4. Building the Plan

Using the results of the team's analysis to go from the general to the specific by confirming directions and establishing goals as springboards for designing effective strategies and tactics and setting measurements for success

5. Implementation

Undertaking projects (usually) outside routine administrative assignments

6. Control and Follow Up

Keeping regular track of progress and modifying plans as appropriate both to establish how far you have come and as a basis for next year's planning

Competitive Strategy Development Process

How to Get Where You Want to Go with What You Have or Can Get

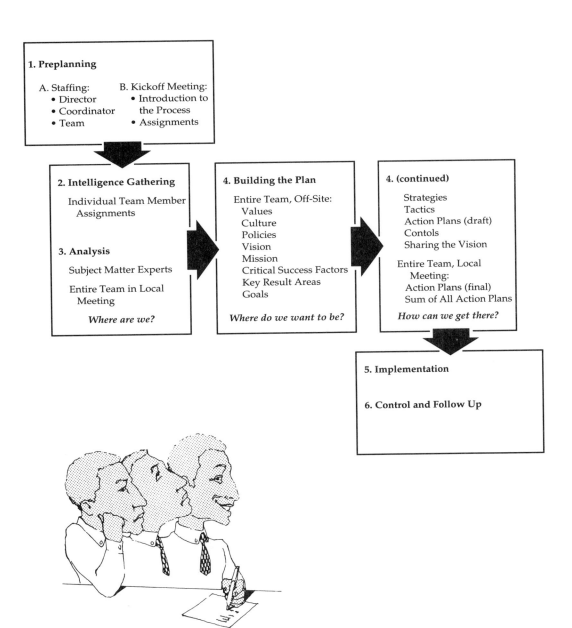

1. Preplanning

A. Staffing:
- Director
- Coordinator
- Team

B. Kickoff Meeting:
- Introduction to the Process
- Assignments

2. Intelligence Gathering

Individual Team Member Assignments

3. Analysis

Subject Matter Experts

Entire Team in Local Meeting

Where are we?

4. Building the Plan

Entire Team, Off-Site:
- Values
- Culture
- Policies
- Vision
- Mission
- Critical Success Factors
- Key Result Areas
- Goals

Where do we want to be?

4. (continued)

- Strategies
- Tactics
- Action Plans (draft)
- Contols
- Sharing the Vision

Entire Team, Local Meeting:
- Action Plans (final)
- Sum of All Action Plans

How can we get there?

5. Implementation

6. Control and Follow Up

BENEFITS

The benefits of thoughtful planning fall into four groups:

Financial Results

Many organizations have found that planning increases revenues or market share or both; some find that planning is the way to save their failing business.

Team Building

Real team building takes place when a group works hard on important matters; few tasks are more critical to an organization than competitive strategy planning, and the people who develop these strategies come to trust and depend on one another in ways that serve the organization from then on.

Organizational Strength

Senior managers often say, after working through the process, that they understand their organization better than ever—sometimes in new ways. Additional benefits are that participants in the process develop as managers by learning to think strategically, and new managers on the team quickly learn about the company in great detail.

Business Reality

Because the planning team analyzes the implications of a variety of information and because many habitual ways of operating are examined critically (often for the first time), the team has a fresh and clear-sighted understanding of exactly how the business stands in relation to the outside world and what strengths and problems the company possesses. Often prejudices about fellow team members dissolve as everyone contributes their best; sometimes, unqualified managers are unmasked.

Process Timeline

The lines on the *Suggested Planning Schedule*[3] shown here represent elapsed calendar time for a typical strategy planning process through its various parts. The values it contains are averages based on experience with hundreds of organizations and will give you a sense of how long your process might take and, especially, what proportion of the time will most likely be spent on each part.

Suggested Planning Schedule

Strategic Planning Schedule	Months After Go-Ahead											
	1	2	3	4	5	6	7	8	9	10	11	12
1. Preplanning	▬											
2. Intelligence Gathering		▬▬▬▬										
3. Analysis					▬							
4. Building the Plan						▪						
5. Implementation							▬▬▬▬▬▬					
6. Control and Follow Up							▬▬▬▬▬▬					

---

3. Reprinted with permission of Dr. Sarah Layton.

Some Questions As You Approach Competitive Strategy Planning

Ask yourself or your team these questions to begin the process of framing a realistic and effective competitive strategy. The easier the answers come, the more ready you are to plan effectively.

1. Who in your company is involved in thinking about the future?

   _____

   _____

   _____

   _____

2. How do you keep track of your competition?

   _____

   _____

   _____

   _____

3. Where do you believe your market is going?

   _____

   _____

   _____

   _____

4. Why is your company successful or why is it not?

   _____

   _____

   _____

   _____

5. How is strategy developed in your company?

_____

_____

_____

_____

6. How does your business compare with projections from a year ago?

_____

_____

_____

_____

7. What level of teamwork exists in your top management group?

_____

_____

_____

_____

8. What kinds of problems do you find in implementing strategy?

_____

_____

_____

_____

S T E P

I

Preplanning

FINDING A DIRECTOR

Planning to Plan

In the same way that planning your competitive strategy is crucial to success, planning to develop your strategic plan is equally important. This section of the book deals with "planning to plan."

There are two parts to every piece of work: *what* you are doing and *how* you are doing it. Experience shows that the best plans are made when the team concentrates on the "what" and a director concentrates on the "how." The person selected for this vital role must be capable in four areas:

✔ They Must Know the Planning Process.

✔ They Must Be Skillful Facilitators.

✔ They Should Be an Unbiased Outsider.

✔ They Must Have Broad Business Knowledge and Experience with Many Organizations.

All this enables the director to ask shrewd questions and help the team synthesize the volumes of intelligence that will be developed.

Knowledge of process means that this person must know the steps of plan building thoroughly and can keep track of the team's progress. Also, this person should be able to extend or abbreviate parts of the process wisely—depending on what is most important to the team while still completing every step of the process and finishing the plan on schedule. This allows team members to remain in their management roles.

Often, a team fails to challenge one another's assumptions by asking unsettling questions. It is the director's job to challenge sacred cows, uncritical assumptions and foggy thinking. Typically, the team learns from the director's behavior to ask difficult but important questions. This willingness to ask such questions is a critical lesson for planning-team members.

FINDING A DIRECTOR (continued)

> ## CASE STUDY: *Learning from Competitors*
>
> Often, an organization's pride leads it to be scornful of competitors. One successful software company, analyzing a major competitor, decided that the competitor's long-term chance of success was small because their software architecture was inferior. Nevertheless, the competitor appeared successful. Probing questions by the planning director elicited the information that although the competitor's products might be technically inferior, they had "user friendliness" that appealed to customers. This insight caused the planning team to reassess the competitor and, ultimately, develop a strategy that focused equally on user friendliness and product technology.

To fulfill this role, the director with broad business experience does *not* need much experience with the business of your particular company. The detachment of a shrewd outside business generalist is a valuable ingredient in the planning process.

A skilled outsider is the most effective choice for director. But sometimes a small organization cannot afford outside help and decides to use one of their own members as directors. This can work if the company chooses a tough-minded person who understands the need to shift back and forth between emphasizing "what" is being done versus "how" it is being accomplished. Look for someone with experience facilitating other kinds of processes, such as problem solving, who will also learn the planning process thoroughly and has a general business outlook. When an internal director is used, it is vital to the planning process (and the director's career) that the whole team—especially the CEO—allow that person to perform his or her assigned role fully without fear of recrimination for asking probing questions.

Finding a Coordinator

The coordinator administers the planning project by seeing that work assignments are done on schedule and that everything is ready for the off-site planning session including transportation, transparencies, notebooks, and the like. Afterward, the coordinator administers the implementation phase since the plan's success depends on persistent follow up and attention to detail. A director who is a member of the organization might also do this job. But the talents needed to direct a planning session differ from those needed to keep track of tasks and make arrangements; not everyone can do both well. Most organizations will be best served by assigning these two roles to different people; the CEO should not undertake either one.

Choosing Team Members

The Planning Team should always include the senior officers of the organization—those who report directly to the Chief Executive Officer. After all, it is their job to set the company's strategic direction. The team should also include those responsible for key operational areas if they are not part of the senior management group in your organization. For example, if the heads of Information Systems or Human Resources are outside that group, consider the value of including them.

Remember: When the planning process is complete, each team member must meet specific measurable goals that support the company's competitive strategy. Choose people with the knowledge, resources and the will to discharge their responsibilities successfully throughout the strategic planning process and afterward. Everyone must be an effective participant.

The larger the team, the longer team meetings will take. Each person is there to contribute and deserves time to be heard. There should be no observers.

DIRECTOR MEETS WITH THE CEO

As the first step in the planning process, the director meets with the CEO to discuss several important items. The first is the reason for conducting a planning session at this time. Reasons range from imminent bankruptcy or uncontrolled growth to the simple sense that the company ought to be doing better. Each suggests different goals and process emphasis.

The director must know the CEO's attitude toward planning. Planning is most effective when the CEO is prepared to rely on the senior management group and endorse new directions based on their collective thinking.

The two should discuss what the planning process is to accomplish in broad terms. The general target might be a strategy for survival, growth or profitability, for increasing market share, or even for selling the company itself. The specifics of these goals, such as actual percentages, come later after analysis at plan-building time.

They should establish the history and results of any previous company planning— what strategic planning has been done and whether or not it was successful. The director is interested in whatever positive or negative expectations the team will bring into the strategic planning process. For example, a poor experience may have left them suspicious or discouraged, or a partial effort may have given them a head start on intelligence gathering.

Another topic is the composition of the planning team, the special contributions to be expected from each, and the relationships among them. The director and CEO need to assign work groups and leaders based on individual talent and experience. Also, it is useful for the director to have the CEO's perceptions about the dynamics of the management team—partly to keep the process smooth and partly to compare what really happens with the CEO's expectations.

The director and CEO should establish the planning schedule from the Preplanning Meeting through the start of Implementation.

The Team Meeting

Every project starts with a kickoff meeting when the CEO introduces team members to the goals of the project, their roles and responsibilities, how the work will be organized and what the rewards or penalties may be. In addition, the director must explain the planning process and train individuals in intelligence gathering and strategic thinking.

This meeting takes about a half day during which the director tells the team about the planning process and their parts in it. The topics that must be covered are presented in brief here; the chapters that follow give specifics.

► The President or CEO begins the meeting by endorsing the importance of developing a competitive strategy for the company and noting that the team here assembled has been carefully chosen to do this vital work—no one else is determining the future of the company.

► The director describes the process of developing a competitive strategy from Preplanning through Control and Follow Up using the pyramid[4] shown here to illustrate how each part builds on previous parts.

Competitive Strategy Team Planning Process

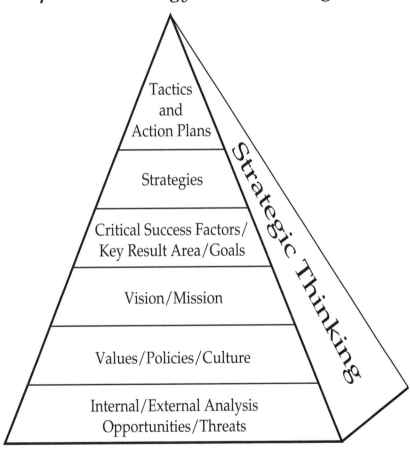

4. Reprinted by permission of the Hamilton Strategic Management Group. © Hamilton Strategic Management Group, 1994.

DIRECTOR MEETS WITH THE CEO (continued)

► The Director next assigns intelligence gathering to the appropriate people by handing out and discussing the forms provided in Step 2, Intelligence Gathering. These forms address areas such as the company's financial situation and history, the market, products and services, employees, customers, competition and corporate culture. Note that the forms provided may not exactly fit your organization. Feel free to modify them to make them more useful.

► The Director then discusses strategic thinking by noting that every team member must play two roles: as a subject matter expert and as a senior manager concerned with the company as a whole. Success demands that typical departmental rivalries be minimized for the good of the enterprise as a whole.

DIRECTOR MEETS WITH INDIVIDUAL TEAM MEMBERS

After the meeting, the director meets individually with each team member to candidly discuss each of their expectations for, and reservations about, the process. Typically, in this discussion, the director addresses unrealistic hopes and fears by describing the experience of other planning teams and clarifies misunderstandings about the tasks of the planning process.

Also, the director makes sure that all team members understand their intelligence-gathering assignments and have the time and resources along with a rough plan for accomplishing the work.

Team Member Tasks and Data-Gathering Worksheets

The worksheets listed here appear in Appendix A. *They can be copied and given to the team members assigned to complete them.* Each worksheet has directions for data gathering.

Director

Planning Organization Worksheet	Form 1

Chief Executive Officer

Environmental Analysis	Form 2
Current Corporate Organization	Form 3

Chief Financial Officer

Financial Analysis:

Profit and Loss Summary (000)	Form 4
Profit and Loss Summary (% of Net Sales)	Form 5
Balance Sheet Summary (000) [Assets/Liabilities and Net Worth]	Forms 6.A and 6.B
Selected Financial Ratios	Form 7
Personnel Data	Form 8

DIRECTOR MEETS WITH INDIVIDUAL TEAM MEMBERS (continued)

Financial History and Current Situation:

The CFO also prepares a summary of the company's financial history and current situation (from the present back three to five years) for presentation at the opening of the strategic planning session. As appropriate, this presentation illustrates key elements from these worksheets with graphs or charts.

Chief Marketing Officer

Marketing Analysis:

Sales Mix   Form 9

For each market segment and competitor:

Market Segment Profile   Form 10

Competitor Strengths and Weaknesses   Form 11

Human Resources Officer

Employee Survey (if available) on job satisfaction, management, ideas for improving operations, training and other job needs

All Team Members

General Organization Data
(In their areas of responsibility)   Form 12

Corporate Climate Assessment   Form 13

Preplanning Guideline

Following the team meeting, participants should be able to articulate goals, timeline, responsibilities, and expectations. The items given here can serve as your guideline.

Team Meeting Summary

- Corporate Planning Goals: _____

  _____

  _____

- Planning Schedule: _____

  _____

  _____

- My Roles and Responsibilities: _____

  _____

  _____

- My Data-Gathering Areas: _____

  _____

  _____

- My Expectations for the Planning Process: _____

  _____

  _____

II

Intelligence Gathering

GATHERING INFORMATION

Gathering data about your customers, your company, your competition, and the world in which you operate can be time consuming but it is enormously rewarding. A realistic understanding of where you stand in relation to all these elements is fundamental to acting wisely in the future. Do the job carefully remembering that inaccurate data can be lethal to your organization.

CASE STUDY: *The Importance of Data*

A manufacturer of small- to medium-size capital goods sold a significant part of their product line through independent agents. Because of their arrangement with the agents, they normally did not have data about the ultimate consumer of this part of their sales. When they tried to determine what drove demand for their products, this lack of data made their information incomplete in this critical area and prevented the team from drawing meaningful insights. A simple alteration of their arrangement solved the problem for the future but they could never recover the history they had lost.

Data vs. Intelligence

Individual facts such as the value of a shipment, the zip code of a customer, or the stock number of a product are *data.* By themselves, these facts are not very useful, but when they are collected and focused, they become *intelligence.* Total shipment values can be gross sales, a collection of customers with the same zip code can indicate the size of a geographic market segment, and total sales by item can show which products are selling well or badly.

Use your experience to decide whether or not the data elements listed on your team members' worksheets in Appendix A will yield useful intelligence. Add others that make sense to you and delete—thoughtfully—those that have no bearing on your business. Decide what you want to learn before you start gathering data.

As you translate data into intelligence, be thorough and try not to make judgments just yet. The interesting thing about intelligence gathering is that unbiased data gathering often yields surprising conclusions.

GATHERING INFORMATION (continued)

CASE STUDY: *An Unexpected Finding*

A medium-sized construction company operated branches in cities throughout the United States. A major source of concern to management was the large profitability variations among branches. Traditional company thinking held that the variability was due almost entirely to individual branch manager quality. They instituted extensive management training programs to solve this (perceived) problem.

However, when they initiated a market analysis of their business highlighting the type of work performed, it became apparent that some branches concentrated on a few types while others tried to "be all things to all people." Further analysis confirmed that those who were more focused generally possessed a strong core competence; their results showed greater customer satisfaction and, not coincidentally, better profits. Apparently the issue was not quality of management as much as the ability to develop and focus on specific core competencies.

While this was, in a sense, a management issue, it was very specific and much easier to address than the broad range of management skills previously under study.

A long-term competitive strategy founded on developing and focusing on individual branch core competencies quickly led to profit improvement as the poorly performing branches learned to focus as well as their more successful counterparts.

How Much Is Enough?

The worksheets provided in this book are based on broad experience with many companies. The intelligence they ask for is usually enough for an average organization.

If, during the intelligence gathering phase, you find some data hard, expensive or even impossible to get, begin with the best estimates you can develop internally. Then, wait until analysis or discussion indicates that more exact intelligence is critical and worth taking extraordinary pains to gather before spending time and money to get it.

WHERE TO FIND INFORMATION

Begin with formal company records such as the annual report, regular periodic reports and the histories kept by responsible managers on such matters as maintenance expenses, brand sales and employee turnover. This kind of intelligence is particularly straightforward in the financial area.

Many other items of intelligence such as opportunities, constraints, problems, corporate climate and external influences come from personal observations as you work with customers, fellow employees and suppliers. Sometimes, insights come from reading or watching television. Formal records tend to reflect history; observations about the world around us let us know where we are and suggest new directions.

Often, companies have a great deal of data that simply needs to be gathered and analyzed, such as customer suggestions or complaints, sales trends, exit interviews and the like. If you can be clear about what you want to know, it is surprising how often you can find the intelligence to answer your questions. Customer suggestions, for example, have always been fertile sources of new product ideas; exit interviews point to organizational problems.

You may need professional help or training when you want objectivity—as you would in surveying employees—or if you have a large group to work with. However, much can be done with the resources on hand. For example, if you want to know how many customers buy more than twice a year, you could find out by looking at a year's worth of sales records or by sampling selected customers—which takes some expertise but is fast, cheap and remarkably accurate.

Intelligence Gathering Planning Worksheet

In your current workplace or situation, assume you have been assigned to a team to gather information in your area. How would you answer the following questions?

1. I am responsible for gathering intelligence in these areas:

_____

_____

_____

2. Major questions to be answered are:

_____

_____

_____

3. I will need these kinds of data:

_____

_____

_____

4. This is where I expect to find the data and how I plan to gather it:

_____

_____

_____

5. These people will help me; their assignments appear beside their names:

_____

_____

_____

III

Analysis

THE TWO-LEVEL APPROACH

Intelligence analysis takes hard thinking and some imagination to produce the kinds of results useful in forming competitive strategy. A two-level approach works best.

Level 1 has each Subject Matter Expert (SME) such as a marketing manager or the chief financial officer first analyze the intelligence gathered about their area using experience to understand the material and draw conclusions. These results are written down and shared among the team.

Level 2 has the team gather in a one-day meeting to present their conclusions for everybody to discuss. (Note: All team members will be SMEs but not all SMEs will be team members; for example, the company attorney or the economist might be SMEs but not on the team.) This approach uses SME expertise to screen intelligence into useful conclusions and invites team members from other disciplines to examine these conclusions critically using their general business knowledge and particular point of view. The aim is to avoid blind spots that come from familiarity with an area.

Level 1: Subject Matter Expert's Data Analysis

Each subject matter expert, knowing what is important in their particular area, gathers and analyzes intelligence to get the answers the organization needs. The Marketing Manager must find out, for example, who the customers are, what they buy, and how satisfied they are—to name just a few of the many questions that need answering. Much of this kind of intelligence will be part of an SME's regular job and will be gathered routinely by the SME's staff.

SWOT identification is a key component of intelligence gathering.

THE TWO-LEVEL APPROACH (continued)

Identifying SWOTs

For their own areas, SMEs must identify four elements:

Strengths   What we should be doing that we already do well

Weaknesses   What we should be doing that we fail to do well

Opportunities   Areas where we can expand or improve

Threats   From competition, government, etc., that we must respond to but cannot prevent

Use the code word: "SWOT" to remember this list.

Every SME should be clear about the organization's current *strengths* and *weaknesses,* at least in his or her area of responsibility. These understandings must be written down for the whole planning team.

In addition, SMEs must think about *opportunities:* The Marketing Manager, for example, should have ideas and intelligence about new products, new markets and new customers; the Production Manager should have ideas about productivity; the Human Resources Manager should be thinking about the best ways to hire and train employees in the future. Although much is unknown when we talk about new directions, every SME should at least have reasonable ideas about areas to be researched and approaches to data gathering.

Threats can be identified in either of two ways:

► Known activities such as lawsuits, regulations or competitive initiatives, or

► Problems that might reasonably happen such as strikes at contract negotiating time, bills before the legislature or the loss of a key manager. Also consider natural disasters such as floods, earthquakes, etc. We call this "creative worrying."

An SME's experience and ingenuity will suggest ways of dealing with visible threats as well as with those that are unseen but that can reasonably be expected.

Identifying PESTs

Opportunities and threats (the "O" and "T" of SWOT) can be found within and outside the company. Most come from four areas outside the organization's control: Political, Economic, Social and Technological. Use the code word "PEST" to remember this list. Each area may threaten the enterprise or present opportunities. For example:

Political	Political realities such as treaties, a new governor or acts of Congress
Economic	Economic factors such as the relation of the dollar to foreign currency, the prime rate and unemployment levels
Social	Social trends such as the aging of the workforce, sentiment against smoking, the Green Movement and immigration
Technological	Technological changes like the declining cost of computing power, the increase of in-flight telephone availability and video conferencing

When you write about opportunities and threats, group them according to the PEST list and note whether they come from inside or outside the company; this will make it easy for the team to understand and think about them.

The CEO's PEST analysis should take the broadest possible view in order to discern outside influences likely to affect the business in the years to come. The CEO's analysis often produces some of the most significant intelligence the team has to address.

THE TWO-LEVEL APPROACH (continued)

CASE STUDY: PEST Analysis

A medium-sized regional bank, serving an essentially rural community, focused on face-to-face, highly personal service as their primary competitive strategy. Their PEST analysis identified several trends that suggested the need for an additional strategy: In recent years, the characteristics of their marketplace had changed to reflect an influx of suburban and urban people seeking "the better life." These people brought a culture and background to the market different from that of traditional customers. They expected technological sophistication from their bank. At the same time, home computing was on the increase as well as the ability to communicate between home computers and the bank.

As they came to understand these developments, the bank team realized that in addition to its branch-oriented face-to-face strategy, it needed a technological strategy. Such a strategy would serve newcomers to the market and their probable demand for electronic banking as opposed to the historic leisurely personal approach.

Without this alteration in strategy—which would entail significant internal culture shifts—the organization would probably be unable to retain its major share of the market.

Level 2: Members' Analysis Session

When every SME has collected data in his or her area and extracted intelligence from it, the whole team meets for an analysis session. This meeting will take at least a day and may take more depending on the amount of material to be analyzed and the number of people on the team. At this meeting, as at the off-site meeting that comes later, individual team members must play two parts at the same time. Primarily, they must be concerned with what is best for the company *as a whole,* while also representing their *area of expertise* (finance, marketing, production, and the like). Corporate thinking is usually the harder of these two. It is critical that all managers learn to play both parts, that is, to think strategically, by the time they gather off-site to build the strategic plan.

As the SMEs present their material, consider these matters:

- Does the hard data and the intelligence derived from it challenge cherished beliefs? After all, reality-based planning is the only kind that succeeds. Be especially alert to surprises and investigate them thoroughly.

- Determine those factors critical to the success of anyone in your business, those few things—usually no more than half a dozen—that you *must* do well in order to succeed. For example, an automobile manufacturer must be concerned with styling, a dealer network and cost control.

- Identity the strengths that help your company succeed, that is, those things which distinguish you as an enterprise in the minds of your customers. These are your core competencies. Match them with the critical success factors for your kind of business to be sure that you have at least a minimum of competency in every critical area, although you may possess additional strengths as well.

- Identify those corporate weaknesses likely to impinge on those factors critical for success.

- Come to agreement on what the financial analysis means.

- Understand the market analysis and develop tentative strategies by market segment.

- Learn what the competition is doing and incorporate this intelligence into your tentative strategies.

- Address all PEST (Political, Environmental, Social and Technological) issues in light of their impact on the company.

Teams find it productive to deal with *internal analysis* ahead of *external analysis;* and then they consider *threats* before *opportunities.* This sequence makes the consideration of opportunities a transition from analysis to planning competitive strategies.

Often, this session produces significant questions that suggest additional data gathering and analysis by individual SMEs. Here too, the team may decide to invest time and money gathering specific additional data originally felt to be too expensive or troublesome.

THE TWO-LEVEL APPROACH (continued)

Prepare a loose-leaf notebook for each participant that includes the material presented by each individual modified on the basis of the team discussion. (We will call this "background intelligence.") Additionally, be sure to include a copy of all conclusions, discussion notes and tentative new directions from flip charts and blackboards (covering internal and external business analyses, threats and opportunities). Suggested tabs for your Competitive Strategy Planning Notebook—First Meeting are:

- Background Intelligence

- Internal Business Analysis

- External Business Analysis

- Threats/Opportunities

(**Note:** Other tabs will be added for the next team meeting.)

Finally, all team members go back to their workplace and use this notebook, their personal notes and their recollection of the meeting to develop ideas about solutions, initiatives and insights into things as they really are.

A Word about the Analysis Meeting

A great deal of concentrated thinking has to be accomplished here, and most people will find it a challenge to be alert throughout the whole meeting. The agenda outline shown here allots time proportioned for each segment of a single-day meeting. Note that if the team is large or the material complex, the meeting might take longer. The director of the meeting must watch the clock, dividing the time fairly among participants and topics and not forgetting breaks for refreshments and lunch. Notice that in a one-day meeting for a team of six, each person has only a half hour (within the Background Intelligence segment) for presentation and team commentary.

First Meeting Agenda Outline

- Purpose of Meeting by CEO (½ hr.)

- Background Intelligence Presentations by SMEs and Team Commentary (3½ hrs.)

— Lunch Break —

- Discussion: Internal Business Analysis (1 hr.)

- Discussion: External Business Analysis (1½ hrs.)

- Discussion: Threats/Opportunities (1½ hrs.)

- Next Steps, Assignments, and Conclusion (½ hr.)

Analysis Worksheet

For your records, list the areas of expertise in your organization and then write the name of the SME for each area. After your Analysis Meeting, write out your responses to the following questions.

1. What SWOTs (Strengths, Weaknesses, Opportunities and Threats) exist in your area of expertise?

   _____

   _____

   _____

   _____

2. What SWOTs do you see in the company outside your area of expertise?

   _____

   _____

   _____

   _____

3. What are the PEST (Political, Economic, Social and Technological) opportunities and threats in your area of expertise?

   _____

   _____

   _____

   _____

4. What are the PEST (Political, Economic, Social and Technological) opportunities and threats *outside* your area of expertise?

_____

_____

_____

_____

5. After the Analysis Meeting, I've found I need to gather more intelligence about these areas:

_____

_____

_____

_____

S T E P

IV

Building the Plan

PREPARING FOR THE PLANNING SESSION

After the local analysis meeting, the team gathers off-site to build the competitive strategy plan. We recommend going off-site as experience shows that planning sessions held on-site tempt participants to try conducting some business as usual; the telephone is an especially troublesome interruption. When planning competitive strategy is new and difficult, managers find it more comfortable to retreat to familiar tasks. Nevertheless, some organizations must—or feel they must—plan competitive strategy locally.

In such cases, it is vital to success that the Director ask the team to establish rules about when and how messages can be delivered to participants and when and for how long managers can leave the meeting. A useful arrangement for messages is to have a message board *outside* the meeting room where messages wait until the team takes a break. In addition, the CEO can establish a norm of handling business outside the session by setting an example of only taking or making calls during breaks and meals.

Advantages of Off-Site Meetings

Managers who have never experienced an off-site meeting may think of such sessions as vacations or rewards, that is, places where no one works very hard and where there is a little too much to eat and drink. Perhaps this is true of gatherings designed specifically to reward performance but Competitive Strategy Planning Sessions differ profoundly from this stereotype.

Competitive Strategy Planning Sessions focus on working out the future of the organization in a process that absorbs the time and energy of participants. It is not unusual to find groups gathering in the evening compelled by the day's discussion to revisit or expand on their conclusions. They rework their numbers to be sure that they can deliver what they promised. These sessions work best away from headquarters for several reasons.

PREPARING FOR THE PLANNING SESSION (continued)

First, the team is away from interruptions. The daily busy-ness of running the company leaves little time for strategic thinking. Urgent tasks with deadlines always preempt important tasks since the latter usually have no deadlines. At the off-site session, there is nothing to do but think strategically and everyone needed is there. So, the work gets done.

Besides, if absolutely necessary, there is always the telephone and fax machine.

Second, the off-site environment encourages the management team members to see themselves as part of a larger whole. Every individual on the planning team, except the Chief Executive Officer, must act in two capacities to make the Competitive Strategy Planning Session successful: Each must represent his or her own area of the company (finance, production, etc.) as well as consider what is best for the entire company. Often, the CEO's point of view is new even to senior-level managers who have spent years in particular disciplines and who normally negotiate with one another for people and money. Moving the session away from the office gives everyone a fresh start and an imperative to work for what is best for the business rather than what is best for their division.

THE PLANNING SESSION

This meeting can take from two to four days depending on the complexity of the business and the size of the team. By this time, the team has gathered whatever additional intelligence was needed and has thought about the values, policies and culture of the organization. Shown here is a sample agenda for a three-day meeting. You might need to adjust the schedule somewhat for your organization to ensure that each element gets the time it requires and address all topics.

DAY ONE	**DAY TWO**	**DAY THREE**
Purpose of Meeting by CEO	Critical Success Factors and Key Result Areas	Tactics and Action Plans (cont.)
Presentations and Discussion of New Intelligence Since Last Meeting	Goals	Controls
Values, Culture and Policies	Strategies	Sharing the Vision
Vision	Tactics and Action Plans	Conclusion
Mission		

At the outset of this meeting, additional notebook tabs (the first four were provided at the first meeting) should be provided as follows:

- Values/Culture/Policies
- Vision
- Mission
- Critical Success Factors
- Key Result Areas

- Goals
- Strategies
- Tactics and Action Plans
- Controls
- Sharing the Vision

THE PLANNING SESSION (continued)

Participants can file in this notebook all material gathered for the planning session and all material developed during this session and the last. When complete, the notebook contains your organization's competitive strategy and tactics plus all the intelligence and thinking behind it: a valuable asset that is probably *company confidential.*

Values, Policies and Culture

When the team returns to the workplace to implement the tactics determined at this meeting, they need to be clear about the organization's "shalts" and "shalt nots." That is, what most people believe is important (*values*), those things we do not do (*policies*), and therefore, what kind of a group we are (*culture*). If tactics do not fit culture, you and your people will not execute them.

Values are things like:

- Level of quality
- Level of service
- Organizational purpose
- Style

- Attitude toward employees
- How hard we work
- Integrity

Policies are limits on activity like:

- Operating in the continental United States only
- Not doing business with the government
- Always choosing the low bidder

Values plus policies equals culture: the kind of organization we are. Some organizations take time in this meeting to develop a creed (which differs from the mission statement described later in this chapter because a creed describes the beliefs of the great majority of the people in the organization while a mission statement is strictly business).

The turbulence of daily living and working absorbs our attention and distracts us from important goals. Urgent things with deadlines that have to be done soon (the weekly report, making a presentation) crowd out important things that usually have no deadlines (learn a foreign language, make a will, establish a research facility). A clear vision steadily reminds us of our long-range goals and ambitions, giving us a star to steer by.

Why a Vision Is Important

Your vision describes where the team wants their organization to be at some future time, say ten years from now. The exact number of years is not as important as choosing a point distant enough so that the team can think about the organization relatively free from current concerns. Experience shows that too short a time frame for the vision usually leads to something that is essentially nothing more than an improved version of the current situation—not the quantum leap forward necessary to energize the organization. A vision should say something about these topics, usually in a fairly general way. Before beginning, you might want to read the filled-out example given on page 48.

> ### *Company Name*
> ### *Vision 2005*
>
> **1.** Sales Volume and Profitability
>
> **2.** Markets to Be Served
>
> **3.** Products/Services to Be Offered
>
> **4.** Relation to Customers and the Marketplace
>
> **5.** Number and Types of Employees
>
> **6.** Core Competencies to Keep or Establish

THE PLANNING SESSION (continued)

Here is an example of the full-length vision statement for a hypothetical company, Contrex Custom Devices, Inc.

Contrex Custom Devices, Inc.
Vision 2005

1. **Sales Volume and Profitability**—By the year 2005 Contrex will gross $165M in sales (35–40% government and 60–65% private industry); net profits of 12%.

2. **Markets to Be Served**—Contrex will continue to serve vehicle manufacturers such as automobiles, aircraft, trucks, power boats, and mass transit.

3. **Products/Services to Be Offered**—We will design and manufacture custom subassemblies using standard elements (motors, fasteners, connectors, etc.) when possible.

4. **Relation to Customers and the Marketplace**—Our *customers* will expect us to solve difficult engineering problems by blending a broad range of expertise in all engineering disciplines with considerable creativity—we will always be designing and piloting things that have never been built before. We will extend the efforts of (and compete with) customer in-house engineering.

   We will differentiate ourselves in the *marketplace* by being the best at producing novel and highly useful products that can, subsequently, be manufactured at reasonable cost; we will charge a premium for design work but price manufactured products competitively.

5. **Number and Types of Employees**—Our scientist/engineer/designer teams will continue to be the core of the business; by 2005 there will be 10–12 teams of 6–8 people each. Administrative management will be minimized and should grow no larger than one manager for every 10 design team people—this includes all levels of management, especially top management. Manufacturing management should stabilize at about 30 and production workers at 400.

6. **Core Competencies to Keep or Establish**—Our core competence will be solving functionality problems made difficult by constraints of space, temperature, cost, or time, for example, using effective teams of interdisciplinary members with a talent for creative thinking.

This full-length vision, after additional input and wordsmithing, should be communicated throughout the company. Keep and publish this full-length vision. Your people make decisions all day long based on available facts and influenced by their own values. Their behavior can be represented by this diagram:

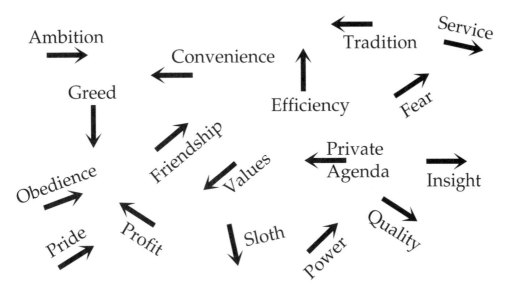

Decision Making without a Corporate Vision

The organization with a unifying vision looks like this single arrow (representing the vision) that contains the employees' individual arrows *all pointing in the same direction.*

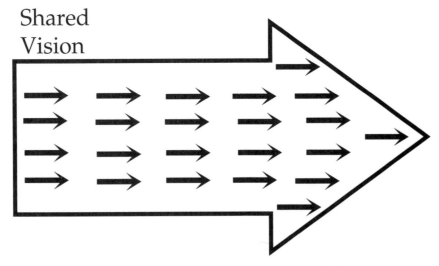

Decision Making with a Corporate Vision

THE PLANNING SESSION (continued)

An effective vision guides everybody's decisions every day and has these characteristics:

- ► **Leader Initiated.** Top management's job is to develop the company's vision; no one else can or will do this.

- ► **Shared and Supported.** Everyone must understand the vision; it cannot be a management secret (remember the arrows).

- ► **Comprehensive and Detailed.** Details make a vision concrete even when broadly stated.

- ► **Positive and Inspiring.** The more important and uplifting the vision, the more people will be energized by it and willing to stretch to meet its goals.

Think how many of these characteristics were met by the vision statement that rallied so many Americans in support of the first space program:

> *I believe that this nation should commit itself to achieving the goal, before this decade is out, of landing a man on the moon and returning him safely to earth.*[5]

> —John F. Kennedy

Another characteristic of visions is that they often contain values, as in this part of General Electric's vision: "A passion for excellence; a hatred of bureaucracy."

If time and talent allow, someone on your team could produce a short, memorable, inspiring version that emphasizes the main points of the vision. For example, using the Contrex statement given in the full-length example, the short version might be:

> *Contrex will grow and prosper, delighting its customers by producing elegant solutions to very difficult technical problems using a team-based approach that combines wide technical expertise and experience with practical creativity. And we will manufacture what we design.*

---

5. Upon the signing of a joint statement by Lockheed Aircraft Corporation and the President's Committee on Equal Employment Opportunity, May 25, 1961.

Mission

Your mission statement tells what business you are in and how you plan to act every day—that is, excellently—to achieve your vision. It is the essential counterweight to the ten-year vision: Visioning without acting is just dreaming and acting without a vision can lead anywhere. Both together will take your company wherever the team wants to lead it. Where vision provides a long-term focus, mission directs the organization for the next three to five years, recognizing what needs to be done immediately to achieve the objectives of the vision.

Generally, the mission should state these things:

- What Business You Are In

- Products and Services

- Customers

Here is an example of a well-thought-out mission statement (examples follow in parentheses):

> ### A Mission Statement
>
> *The mission of Smith Corporation is to become the dominant supplier of user-installed aftermarket automotive products (the business). Our customers in North America own small and medium-sized vehicles of both domestic and foreign manufacture (customers). We will achieve dominance by offering products that combine ease of installation with competitive quality and are sold at an above-average price. These will include performance-improvement equipment, tools, novelties such as comfort items and appearance enhancers (products and services). Our unique competence will be an unsurpassed understanding of the needs of our customers and this will drive everything we do.*

THE PLANNING SESSION (continued)

What Business You Are In

Be particularly careful deciding what business you are in. The railroads got into trouble by limiting themselves to the railroad business; when they understood that they were in the transportation business, we began to see piggyback trucks on flatcars and a return to profitability. Professional sports teams understand they are in the entertainment business, which broadens their scope of activity. On the other hand, beware of broad definitions that provide little direction to the organization. A distillery defining itself as being in the "beverage" business could devote resources to investigating coffee, tea or milk—probably not good diversifications. In this case, a phrase like "social beverages" probably would be more meaningful.

Customers

Be clear about your customers so that everything you plan to do gives them the same reassuring message: "This company sells your kind of product/service."

Selecting the customers you intend to serve can be your most significant decision. It is part of a circular process in which core competencies determine initial products or services . . . which defines customers . . . who in turn suggest additional products and services. And these new products or services may require changes in core competencies. All together, these determine the shape of the company: staffing, organization, strategies, even location. You must be clear about who your customers are, that you can reach them, that what you offer them fills real needs both now and in the future, and finally that you can bring them these things at a price they can and will pay in preference to competing methods of satisfying their needs.

Products and Services

Similarly, be alert to the need to offer new products and services but be certain you truly understand whatever business you enter. New products, mergers, and acquisitions have been the Waterloo of many companies that did not know what they were getting into.

Critical Success Factors and Key Result Areas

In Step 3, Analysis subject experts were asked to identify the factors critical for your business. These are those few things your company—in fact any company in your business—must do well to prosper. Key Result Areas (KRAs) describe what you will measure in your company to be sure of satisfying the imperatives of these critical success factors.

If a steady stream of new products is critical to your business, for example, then everything about new products could become key result areas to be measured periodically. For example, this could be the number of new product ideas submitted to a screening committee, the number of new products introduced to the marketplace every year and new product success. However, organizations do best when they concentrate on a few strategic KRAs and leave subordinate KRAs to functional managers. In this new product example, a single KRA summarizing what the team wants to measure might be product mix—what percent of our product line is less than two years old and what is the profitability of those new products?

When the company performs well in meeting the requirements of a KRA, it needs to keep up the good work. But when your company's performance differs from what a KRA study suggests is optimal, strategic attention is needed. For these areas, establish measurable ideal objectives as planning targets. For instance, an objective might be that new products make up half the product mix within the next two years.

Goals

The next step is to see what goals the team can commit to. Attempt to set realistic goals for the next three to five years for your organization. Build some stretch into your goals—organizations sometimes tend to underachieve. With your goals as a guide, the data you gather will provide useful intelligence about progress or the lack of it.

Using the *Competitive Strategy Development: From Critical Success Factor to Action Plans* (provided here) as an example, you can see the progression from a single Critical Success Factor to a set of Action Plans. (Use this chart while reading the rest of this section to understand how competitive strategies develop from the general to the specific in a logical flow.)

Competitive Strategy Development: From Critical Success Factor to Action Plans (New Products)

Critical Success Factor	Key Result Area and Measures	Strategy	Tactics	Action Plans
Continuous successful new product introductions	Product mix (what percent of product line is less than two years old? What is profit contribution of new products?)	Increase number of successful new products in the product mix by learning to understand what the market wants and needs	Focus employees on new product identification and development	Set up profit sharing system
			Listen actively to customers	Refine development process in R&D
			Understand marketplace	Establish screening committee
			Watch competitive product offering	Train product managers in development and introduction of new products
			Establish new product oversight committee	Set up routine competitive data gathering process
				Establish intelligence recording system
				Establish score-keeping system
				Set up focus groups

Read this example from left to right remembering that these lists are not exhaustive.

Notice that the Critical Success Factor generates a single stategic Key Result Area which, in turn, leads to a single Strategy. Strategies tell, at a policy level, *what* is to be done; Tactics say, more specifically, *how* Strategies are to be executed. Thus, one Strategy can lead to several Tactics, and each Tactic can lead to many Action Plans. Action Plans are the six-month (or less) projects that execute Tactics and Strategies and fulfill the goals of Key Result Areas.

Since new products is the key result area in our example, goals might include, among others:

- The number of products introduced within the last 16 months as a percent of all active products

- The profitability of new products compared with established products

- The number of new products in the development pipeline

These goals form the basis for all future plans and must be endorsed by the team, especially the managers, responsible for specific results.

The subteam approach recommended to develop the vision, discussed earlier in this section, can be useful in goal setting. Divided into subteams, all team members become active participants in the goal-setting process, thereby ensuring involvement and commitment by the leaders of the various sections of the organization. Make sure that all goals are established as "our goals" by the managers involved.

Strategies

Strategies say *what* you are going to do to achieve the goals set in your key result areas, and tactics say *how* you are going to do it. Typically, each goal requires a separate strategy unless creativity or luck combine to allow one strategy to achieve more than a single goal. For example, if your goal is having new products represent half of your product mix within two years, then a strategy might be:

> *Develop processes for identifying, developing and bringing to market profitable new products that fit our mission; support this effort with appropriate people and resources.*

Strategies are, by nature, established at a general level. At this stage in the process, you are identifying areas where priority effort must be expended (new product development) and directing the nature of that effort (developing processes and allocating resources).

As a rule, there should be few strategies—five to seven are usual. That is not to say that these are the only things the team has identified as being desirable to do. Rather, it says that, of the many things identified, these are those few things likely to make the greatest difference and therefore the things to which the organization will devote its scarce resources. An overwhelming tendency is to undertake too many strategies. It is hard to decide not to do something which, on the surface, seems desirable—prioritizing strategies fully tests the mettle of management. A competitive strategic plan that undertakes more work than the resources of the company can support is a recipe for failure.

THE PLANNING SESSION (continued)

Tactics and Action Plans

Since tactics are the *how* of planning, be specific about exactly what is to be done to realize every strategy. Tactics for the new product strategy presented in our example might be divided into:

- Identifying New Products

- Developing Promising New Product Ideas

- Bringing New Products to Market

There will always be at least one tactic to support each strategy and often more. Similarly, each tactic leads to one or more action plans. Action plans are defined as the projects the organization will undertake to shape its future. Action plans have three parts:

#1 A description of the plan connecting it to the tactic, strategy, goal and key result area, and critical success factor that it supports

#2 A schedule of major tasks with target dates and individual responsibilities

#3 Estimates of the time and money required over the life of the action plan and the expected payback over some appropriate period, such as the next three to five years

The tactic of identifying new products might generate a single action plan or several action plans depending on the size of the effort. As a rule, action plans should take no more than six months to accomplish and shorter plans are better. Your team's knowledge of the realities of your business must guide you.

In the period between this meeting and the next, the teams responsible for executing the action plans identified here will use the worksheets provided in this book to describe each action plan fully (by identifying it, laying out its major milestones, and presenting its costs and benefits). For now, at this off-site meeting, the title of each action plan, a brief description, and best estimates of target dates, costs and benefits are sufficient. When the planning team returns to the workplace, these must be refined and the worksheets completed by the people who will implement those action plans. Once again, the team concept ensures the involvement and commitment so essential to successful achievement. Where an action plan affects multiple functions within the organization, ensure that the team preparing the plan has members from each affected function.

All members of the planning team commit to championing action plans in their area of organizational responsibility. First each champion selects teams to develop action plans in the champion's area of responsibility. Once an action plan has been approved, the champion will provide resources for the project managers responsible for each action plan, clear away red tape, and display a continuing interest in project progress. As an example, the first action plan in developing a competitive strategy for your organization is conducting a strategic planning session. The CEO is champion, and the coordinator is project manager.

THE SUM OF ALL ACTION PLANS

Once all the assigned teams have written their action plans in the period following this off-site session, the planning team will reconvene to review these plans. (This session is best held on-site so that action plan project managers can present their plans and answer questions without having to travel.) At this session, the team focuses on the following questions:

- Does each action plan effectively address the strategies and goals it is designed to implement?

- Are the steps, schedules and requirements for people and money realistic?

- Can all action plans together be staffed and funded from available resources or do some need to be delayed until key resources are free?

- When all action plans are consolidated, does the resulting financial outlook for the organization make sense?

A useful tool for addressing the last question is the Action Plan Matrix (Appendix B of this book), which shows the sum of all action plans for the next three years. The Director makes a large matrix on the wall of the conference room using a blackboard or sheets of flip chart paper. Then the Director simply lists all action plans.

Next, the team determines the company's base business for each of the next three years—that is, the business that can be expected without special efforts such as the strategies and tactics discussed at the off-site meeting. Put these three values on a flip chart.

As each action plan is presented and discussed, record on the matrix its costs, benefits and net value (the difference between costs and benefits). When all action plans have been presented, add all net values to the base business year by year and see if the action plans meet the goals set at the off-site meeting. For safety, total values should exceed goals by at least 25–30 percent. If they fall short, more action plans are required. If resources and time are limited, goals might have to be revised.

Some kinds of action plans have costs only. These arise, for example, from the need to comply with government mandates.

Controls

Controls measure progress and tell if you are winning or losing. They are the data that give you decision-making information. Near the end of this three-day session, the team needs to develop and agree on a system of controls:

► Action plan controls (presented in Step 6: Control and Follow Up) will tell you whether spending is going according to plan or progress is going according to schedule but say nothing about how effective the results of the project may be.

► Goals measure the results of executing tactics (that is, one or more action plans) as part of a strategy, and tell how well each tactic is accomplishing what it was designed to do.

The control system, managed by the Coordinator, should include a procedure for keeping the planning team informed and having them meet periodically to review progress. The purpose of such a meeting is twofold: to evaluate progress and to make decisions, as necessary. Inevitably, actual results deviate from plans. The team must address variations and decide when action is required. Hold such meetings monthly until the team decides that less frequent meetings will be adequate.

Sharing the Vision

Planning competitive strategy is foremost the responsibility of senior management but executing it is everybody's job. The last step in this off-site meeting must be to plan a strategy for sharing the vision and mission with everyone in the organization. Typically employees worry about what has been going on at this senior-level meeting; you must let them know immediately what has been decided and what it means to them. Many will be involved in implementing action plans. Some of the information will be corporate confidential, but to the extent possible keep everyone informed of plans and progress. Use what you have discovered about the organization's climate to help in designing this sharing.

Building the Plan: A Preparation Worksheet

Prepare yourself for the off-site meeting by answering these questions.

1. What are the company's core values?

_____

_____

2. What are the company's core policies?

_____

_____

3. What kind of an organization do we belong to?

_____

_____

4. What business are we in?

_____

_____

5. What are our products or services, and whom do we sell to?

_____

_____

6. What would you like to see in the company's Vision?

_____

_____

7. What should the company's Mission be, day to day?

_____

_____

8. Every company in our business must do well in a few areas to survive and prosper; these are:

_____

_____

9. Key result areas for our particular business and goals for those areas are:

_____

_____

10. I will propose that our core strategies be:

_____

_____

11. Effective tactics to accomplish the goals of these strategies should be:

_____

_____

12. The names of proposed action plans associated with each of these tactics and the project managers who might be assigned to them are:

_____

_____

13. Useful ways of sharing all the team developments with the rest of the company are:

_____

_____

S T E P

V

Implementation

MANAGING PROJECTS

Planning is about what we will do *now* to make the *future* what we want it to be, thus implementation of action plans is the critical next step in executing competitive strategy. Action plan projects need championing because many fall outside people's regular duties and they need a special kind of management because projects differ from routine administrative work in important ways.

Of course, some jobs actually consist largely of projects that fit the description of an action plan, such as software development or new product introduction, but even the people in such jobs will find action plans replacing or being added to current assignments.

This part of the book presents ideas about managing projects. Although the projects described in your action plans will vary in complexity, the concepts described in this section apply to all projects. The difference is that the more complex the project, the more strictly these concepts should be adhered to and documented. Whereas simple projects usually can be managed well with action plan worksheets alone, for complex projects, use project management software to establish and maintain schedule control rather than simply relying on worksheets.

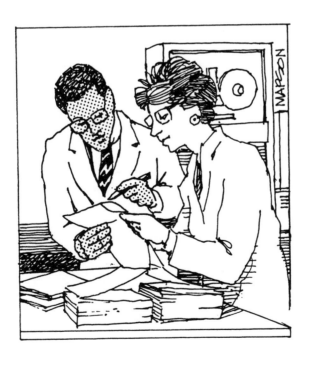

MANAGING PROJECTS (continued)

Project Work vs. Routine Work

Key elements of project work are deadlines, novelty, pressure and change. Key elements of normal work are regularity, efficiency and fluctuating pressure. The table below suggests other differences.

PROJECT WORK	ROUTINE WORK
Definite start and end	Continuous process
Well-defined objective	Periodic deliverables
Unique product	Routine product
High pressure	Varying pressure
Team of many skills	Fewer skills in work group
Method plus creativity more valuable than business experience	Business experience most valuable
Cuts across organizational boundaries	One organization
Team concentrates on goals	Must deal with all staff issues
Frequent change	Moderate change
Staff assigned only for project duration	Permanent staff
Project manager might not have direct authority over all resources needed	Most resources required are contained in unit

© Alfred B. Hurd

What Project Managers Do

Projects are undertaken when it is important to do something new—efficiency comes later. Project managers:

- Plan the project and replan as necessary to account for changes in scope, resources or team members

- See that the work gets done on schedule; this is the part of the job most like general management

- Build and work closely with the project team whose members often come from areas outside the project manager's expertise

- Connect the project with their own management, usually the planning team champion

- Serve the project's customer intelligently managing change and expectations constantly while producing effective results

The best candidates for project managers have four areas of competence:

- They are good at thinking—that is, planning, problem solving and information gathering

- Their self-confidence lets them operate successfully in the uncertain project environment and keeps their tempers even

- They understand and endorse the business purpose of the project they are managing and can make decisions accordingly

- They are wonderful with people: motivating, negotiating and dealing with conflict

The planning team, as project champions, should look for managers skillful in at least three out of four of these areas and at least competent in the fourth.

Project managers may actually do little project work themselves—they are there to *manage*. This means that they balance, and sometimes reprioritize, the three demands of any project—to be as good as possible, given the constraints of time and money available.

MANAGING PROJECTS (continued)

How Much Time to Spend

Experience shows that between 5 and 15 percent of the time planned for a project should be management time; that is, time in addition to the time spent producing deliverables. The average is 10 percent. For example, a project with a team of 10 full-time people should have an 11th person full-time as project manager. By the same arithmetic, one person can manage two five-person teams . . . or one five-person team half time and do project work during the other half.

If the project is complex or if it involves many parts of the organization, it will take more management; if it is simple and the team comes entirely from one department, it may take less. In any case, there should be only one project manager, although some clerical work, such as time reporting, can be delegated.

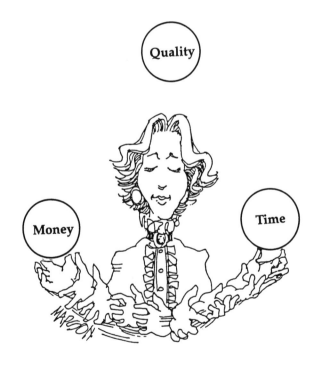

THE TEN ESSENTIALS OF PROJECT PLANNING

It is the project manager's responsibility to anticipate what has to be done and act accordingly. Successful project planning addresses these 10 items:

1. **Clarify goals and objectives.**   The initial responsibility of the planning team's project champion is to explain why this project has been launched and its importance to the business.

2. **List all tasks in detail.**   Projects miss their deadlines more often because of tasks not planned for than for poor estimates. Include *all* the tasks.

3. **Identify dependencies among tasks.**   Some tasks must precede others, and some can be done in parallel with others; use a software package to define and keep track of all the tasks and their dependencies.

4. **Describe the people and resources needed.**   Selecting the team and defining special tools, training or facilities follows understanding of the scope and kind of work to be done.

5. **Estimate task times and costs.**   Make estimates after the team has been selected; some people work faster than others. The sum of estimated costs is the budget.

6. **Apply a productivity factor.**   No one can work full-time on a project for all sorts of legitimate reasons: meetings, vacation, training, etc. Expect no more than 75 percent of a team member's time to be devoted to project work; in some companies this percent is smaller.

7. **Divide tasks into segments of two weeks or less.**   Each segment must have a deliverable that is clearly either done or not done on its due date. A two-week period is about the right balance between overmanaging a task and allowing the assigned person freedom to accomplish the job as they think best. Also, the project will not be more than two weeks behind if the deliverable is late—probably less since at least *some* work will have been done. Remember: with a 75 percent productivity factor, the 80 calendar hours in two weeks will produce 60 hours of project work.

THE TEN ESSENTIALS OF PROJECT PLANNING (continued)

8. Establish a change budget. Padded estimates lead to trouble; reality-based management is best. To the best estimate of project cost, add from 10–20 percent and assign this figure to the budget. An expected rate of change greater than 20 percent suggests a poorly planned or exceptionally volatile project that probably ought to be reconsidered. Here is an example of budgeting when dealing with a "customer":

> If the Information Systems Department is building an order processing system for the Sales Department, Sales is the "customer." When a change arises from the customer's growing understanding of the features and functions of the project deliverable, from changes in the marketplace, or from some other source, that change must be estimated in terms of its dollar and time cost to the project. Then the customer decides whether or not to include the change in the project. If the answer is "yes," then the money for the change is transferred to the project budget which the project manager manages.

9. Establish a delivery process. This point is tied closely to item #7. The process of delivering a project's objectives is the delivery of one small element after another to the client. There should be no major surprises and certainly no single large delivery at the end of a long period.

10. Consider potential problems. To a remarkable degree, managers can head off or prepare for most of the problems likely to trouble a project, but only if problems are identified. The example on the next page illustrates this.

A solid project plan built by following the 10 steps given here powerfully assures project success. Project champions should know that adequate planning saves project time overall. Remember, if the project is even moderately complex—that is, if it has more than about 50 individual tasks—use project management software to establish and control it.

EXERCISE: *Identifying Problems*

Follow this example as if you were managing a project to install a custom-made industrial robot:

► Identify each major possible threat to the project; for example, the robot does not arrive on time.

► Name all reasonable causes for this problem: it is not built in time for shipment date, it is not shipped on time or there is a transportation breakdown.

► For each cause, determine what can be done to *prevent* its happening; some creativity may be needed here. For this example, consider the "not built on time" threat. You could stay in touch with the vendor's order processing and production people—perhaps through a customer representative—and you could also offer a bonus for on-time delivery and/or assess a penalty for late delivery.

► For each cause decide how you will know if the problem has occurred or not, and determine how best to protect the project if the problem does occur despite protective measures.

Take the late shipment problem as an example. First of all, staying in touch with the vendor's people is vital. Use what you learn from the vendor's people to assess where their progress actually stands relative to your need for the robot. If you are worried, you might even visit their plant and see if their project manager is planning effectively.

If it looks as if the robot will be late, revisit your own project progress and decide whether or not the delivery date set when the robot was ordered should be changed. Perhaps the robot is not on the critical path and you have slack time. If so, shift the due date, since this robot is one of a kind.

If the delivery date cannot be shifted, assess the impact of its late arrival on the project and see if you can recover lost days by shortening other tasks on the critical path. Otherwise, share the bad news with the project champion as soon as it is inevitable. Be sure to have options to suggest.

Implementation Worksheet

Before answering the following questions, list the Action Plans you are going to champion and name the people who will manage them.

_____

_____

_____

1. How much time do these project managers need to manage their projects adequately?

   _____

   _____

   _____

2. If they have other duties, how much time do these take?

   _____

   _____

   _____

3. What is the total number of hours expected of each project manager? Are there any scheduling problems?

   _____

   _____

   _____

4. When will the project managers meet with you to go over their project plans?

   _____

   _____

   _____

5. What is a realistic productivity factor for my area of this company?

_____

_____

_____

6. Do the project managers have any shortcomings that may cause complications? How will you address these?

_____

_____

_____

7. Which is the most important consideration in the accomplishment of each project—quality, cost, or time spent?

_____

_____

_____

VI

Control and Follow Up

PROJECT CONTROL

The planning process behind your company's competitive strategy moves from vision and mission to set goals in key result areas. Action plan projects are initiated to meet those goals. This section tells how to ensure that the benefits promised by those action plans develop on schedule.

The Delivery Process for each individual action plan project provides basic information for managing the company's planned competitive strategy. As each two-week (or less) task is accomplished, the project has produced one more deliverable—some are more significant than others but all are valuable in the progression. Tracking project progress shows whether or not strategic initiatives are developing on schedule.

The Weekly Project Report form presented here has been designed so that project team members can fill it out quickly and project managers can make rapid summaries. The various items on the form are explained as follows:

► **Accomplishments**
Each reporting team member uses the task code assigned to every two-week (or less) task to tell what they accomplished and when. Remember, every task was planned with a *done/not done* measure; tasks reported as accomplished have passed the *done* test (specification complete, milling machine hardwired on shop floor, etc.). The project manager uses individual reports to check off completed tasks from the overall project plan. Actual completion dates provide project history and insight into estimating accuracy.

► **Planned Tasks**
This is simply a list of what the person reporting plans to do next week. The project manager verifies that these tasks are appropriate in light of the project schedule.

► **Problems Encountered**
Developing new things never progresses smoothly. The project manager needs to know what major problems have been encountered and where they stand. Have they been solved? Should the project manager or champion become involved? Is a pattern emerging?

► **Potential Problems**
Project managers are vitally concerned with identifying and heading off potential problems; team members need to extend their project manager's vision by pointing out trouble in time to neutralize it.

PROJECT CONTROL (continued)

WEEKLY PROJECT REPORT

Name: *Chris Davies*   **Week Ending:**   **7/10**

Accomplishments

Task ID/Task Name/Date Complete

1874	*Approved bubble wrap specs.*	*7/8*
1875	*Prep'd wrap purchase order.*	*7/10*

Planned Tasks for Next Week

Task ID/Task Name/Planned Start Date

1876	*Design outer box.*	*7/13*
1877	*Design 12-pack.*	*7/15*

Problems Encountered

Description/Current Situation

Solving the failure of No. 3 wrapping machine took half a day from project; back on track through overtime.

Potential Problems

Description/Prevention/Protection/Information

Bubble Wrap Co. in contract negotiations may lead to strike. Can't prevent. Will have alternative supplier ready.

GOALS

When complete, some projects produce results immediately (for instance, cutting manufacturing costs by 2 percent). Others establish initiatives that should become profitable (new product launch, training programs and so on), but whose value remains to be seen. The results of all projects added together can be compared with key result area goals set during the planning process. These should be evaluated according to the timetable set out during the planning process.

For example, if the *goal* was to increase market share from 12 to 17 percent, employing the *strategy* of introducing five new products during the next eight months, the *tactics* might have included the following *action plans:*

Action Plan #1:   Introduce product A by end of first month.

Action Plan #2:   Introduce product B by end of first six weeks.

Action Plan #3:   Introduce product C by end of third month.

Action Plan #4:   Introduce product D by end of sixth month.

Action Plan #5:   Introduce product E by end of eighth month.

Assuming that each new product will increase market share 1 percent eight weeks after introduction, then there is a timetable of expected goal achievement that begins two months after product A is introduced and claims an additional 1 percent market share. Thereafter, products B through E will be introduced and will mature in the marketplace until—by the end of the tenth month—all five products have market acceptance and the company's market share is up from 12 to 17 percent.

A similar timetable can be made for every action plan and the aggregate of these timetables will forecast expected progress toward company goals over time.

REGULAR REPORTING

In the same way that action plan projects need regular weekly reporting, progress toward major corporate goals should be measured regularly. It is a truism of management that what is measured usually improves.

Quarterly meetings of the planning team are the minimum number needed to keep current with progress toward goals. Probably not everything will go as planned; some initiatives may have to be dropped, others redirected. As action plan champions, the members of the planning team should invite their project managers to present their results and answer questions. It can be a fine learning experience—the planning team will hear the person best qualified to answer questions, and the champions will demonstrate good delegation.

Summary

Planning competitive strategy is not a one-time enterprise. To maintain strategic effectiveness, the management team must meet annually to celebrate progress, analyze problems and modify goals. Typically, they will find themselves enjoying increasingly fruitful discussions as their intelligence gathering grows more and more productive and their ability to think strategically improves. They establish new action plans to succeed the ones completed the year before and formulate ways of sharing good news and bad with the rest of the organization.

Remember, competitive strategic planning requires practice over time. Experience suggests that a team needs at least three annual sessions to become really proficient. The good news is that team members learn a great deal in the first session, enough to construct a potent competitive strategy; even those who had reservations at first end up looking forward to the next year's session.

Control and Follow Up Worksheet

1. For the action plan projects you are championing, list their project managers and the dates when they will report progress to you:

_____

_____

_____

_____

_____

2. For each action plan for which you are responsible, list the first date each is to have a measurable goal accomplished—and identify what that goal is:

_____

_____

_____

_____

_____

3. The Competitive Strategy Planning Team will reconvene on this date:

_____

_____

_____

_____

_____

Appendixes

APPENDIX A

Planning Organization Worksheet

Form 1

Team Member Name and Title	Address and Telephone/Fax Numbers
Director:	
Coordinator:	
Team Members:	

Environmental Analysis   *Form 2*

List here the key factors external to your organization—and outside your
control—that help or hinder your survival. Include those that now affect you
and those of growing importance over the next three to five years. Categories
are: **P**olitical, **E**conomic, **S**ocial and **T**echnological, abbreviated as P, E, S or T.
You may not need every one.

Factors	Category P, E, S or T	Impact + or −	Comments

Current Corporate Organization

Form 3

An organization's structure should support its purposes, or "Form follows function" as the saying goes. Analyzing the strengths and weaknesses of the current organization gives the team the understanding needed to make changes, as appropriate, to match the organization's newly developed competitive strategic plan.

Record your ideas about all that is effective or ineffective in the current organizational structure, using the questions below as guides and adding whatever other matters are important.

1. Does the structure effectively direct and control operations; are people doing what ought to be done?

_____

_____

_____

2. Is the structure efficient?

_____

_____

_____

3. Are the links between functional areas effective?

_____

_____

_____

4. Is the organization too flat, or are there too many levels?

_____

_____

_____

Current Corporate Organization (continued)

5. Are managers rewarded for the number of people they supervise or for effectiveness?

_____

_____

_____

6. Are there the right number of people in each functional area?

_____

_____

_____

7. Are any vital functions missing?

_____

_____

_____

8. How are changes made to the current organization?

_____

_____

_____

Profit and Loss Summary (000)

Form 4

Percent Increase or Decrease by Year ▶	Year	%INC/ (DECR)	Year	%INC/ (DECR)	Year	%INC/ (DECR)	Estimate Next Year
Net Sales							
Cost of Sales							
Gross Profit							
Selling Expense							
Gen. & Admin. Expense							
TOTAL Expense							
Operating Income							
Other Income/Expenses:							
Interest Income							
Other Income							
Interest Expense							
Other Expense							
Net Profit Before Tax:							
Income Taxes							
Net Profit After Taxes							
Dividends							
Depreciation							

Profit and Loss Summary (000)

Form 5

Percent Increase or Decrease by Year ▶	Year	%INC/ (DECR)	Year	%INC/ (DECR)	Year	%INC/ (DECR)	Year	%INC/ (DECR)	Estimate Next Year
Net Sales	100%		100%		100%		100%		100%
Cost of Sales									
Gross Profit									
Selling Expence									
Gen. & Admin. Expense									
TOTAL Expense									
Operating Income									
Other Income/Expenses:									
Interest Income									
Other Income									
Interest Expense									
Other Expense									
Net Profit Before Tax:									
Income Taxes									
Net Profit After Taxes									
Dividends									
Depreciation									

Balance Sheet Summary (000)

Assets

Form 6A

For Fiscal Year ▶					Estimate for Next Year
Cash					
Marketable Securities					
Accounts Receivable (Net)					
Inventory					
Prepaid Expenses					
Other Current Assets:					
Total Current Assets:					
Land					

Buildings
    Less Reserve for Depreciation
    Buildings Net					

Machinery and Equipment
    Less Reserve for Depreciation
    Machinery and Equipment Net					

Other Assets					
Total Assets:					

Balance Sheet Summary (000)
Liabilities and Net Worth

For Fiscal Year ▶						Estimate for Next Year
Accounts Payable						
Notes Payable						
Current Short-Term Debt						
Accrued Expenses						
Other Current:						
Total Current Liabilities:						
Long-Term Debt						
Total Liabilities:						
Preferred Stock						
Common Stock						
Paid in Surplus						
Retained Earnings						
Total Net Worth:						
Total Liabilities and Net Worth:						

Selected Financial Ratios

For Fiscal Year ▶					Estimate for Next Year	Industry Standards
Current Ratio (CA/CL)						
Total Debt/Net Worth						
Long-Term Debt/Net Worth						
Accounts Receivable/Sales						
Cost of Sales/Inventory						
Gross Profit/Sales						
Pretax Profit/Sales						
Net Profit After Taxes/Sales						
Net Profit After Taxes/Net Worth						
Net Profit After Taxes/Total Assets						
Net Profit After Taxes/Total Capital Employed						
Other Ratios Pertinent to Your Organization:						

Personnel Data

Form 8

For Fiscal Year ▶					Estimate for Next Year
Number of Employees:					
Nonexempt					
Exempt					
Total:					
Average Years of Service					
Employee Turnover Rate					
Number of Employees:					
Per $MM Sales					
Per $MM Total Assets					
Per $MM Net Profit A/T					
Wages, Salaries and Benefits:					
Average Wage Rate—Hourly					
$ Salary, Wages and Benefits/Sales					
$ Salary, Wages and Benefits/Net Profit After Taxes					

Sales Mix

Form 9

The data collected on this sheet show sales of each major product or service classified by whatever categories your organization finds useful. For example, categories might be: major lines of business and distribution channels, market segment and customer class, or geographic area. You probably have particular categories especially for your organization. Use a separate copy of this form for each category, listing on it all products and services appropriate to that category.

Category: _____

Products and Services Year ▶	% of Mix	% of Mix	% of Mix	% of Mix	% of Mix	Next Year's Est. %s

Market Segment Profile

Form 10

The data on this form describe the markets and market segments in which your organization operates. Use a separate copy of this form for each different market or market segment.

Market or Market Segment Description: _____

Applications or Customer Classes: _____

Channels of Distribution: _____

					Next Year's Estimate
Year ▶					
Market Size:					
Units					
Dollars (000)					
Market Rate of Growth (% Annual Change)					
Our Share of Market:					
Units					
Dollars (000)					
Percent					
Major Competitors:	Share %	Share %	Share %	Share %	Share %

Competitor Strengths and Weaknesses   *Form 11*

Use one form for each competitor/product/service combination appropriate to your organization.

Competitor Name: _____

Product/Service: _____

1. List competitor's strengths.

   _____

   _____

   _____

2. List competitor's weaknesses.

   _____

   _____

   _____

3. What strategies is this competitor following?

   _____

   _____

   _____

4. How is your organization responding to this competitor now—if you are—and how should you respond in the future?

   _____

   _____

   _____

General Organizational Data

Every team member should answer the questions on this form on a separate piece of paper and bring them to the first meeting. The data it asks for will fuel your discussions.

1. What core competencies does your organization have? That is, what do you do better than your competition?

2. What other strengths does the organization have?

3. What weaknesses exist within the organization?

4. What major opportunities do you see for your organization in the next few years?

5. What key measurements determine the success of your organization?

6. What difficulties do you foresee for your organization in the next few years?

7. What changes, if any, are needed in the way your organization is structured and managed to make it more effective in the future?

8. What company policies—written and unwritten—affect decision making; should they be changed?

9. What has been the recent strategic emphasis?

10. What are the major strategic issues to be resolved?

11. What other significant matters not noted above should the team consider when it meets?

Corporate Climate Assessment

Form 13

The questions on this form ask you to describe your organization's climate or culture in two ways: first, the way things are done and the values most people agree on *now* and, second, the way you think things ought to be done and the values that ought to be agreed on *for the future* success of the organization.

Listed below are a number of statements that may or may not apply to your particular organization. Using a scale from 1 to 7 please evaluate the degree to which you feel each statement characterizes your organization both now and as it needs to be in the future.

1	=	Strongly disagree; not true at all
2–3	=	Mostly not true
4	=	Neutral; sometimes true, sometimes false
5–6	=	Mostly true
7	=	Strongly agree; very true
?	=	Don't know

	Now	Future
1. Everyone knows the organization's mission.	_____	_____
2. Departmental and personal objectives are set out clearly.	_____	_____
3. The organization is good about communicating with its employees.	_____	_____
4. Operational/production systems are efficient and effective.	_____	_____
5. Information systems are efficient and useful.	_____	_____
6. People are organized in a sensible way.	_____	_____
7. Individual initiative and creativity are encouraged.	_____	_____
8. Teamwork is encouraged.	_____	_____
9. Management seeks input from below before making decisions.	_____	_____
10. We go all out to serve our customers.	_____	_____
11. Customer satisfaction is measured routinely.	_____	_____
12. The quality of our products is excellent.	_____	_____

Corporate Climate Assessment (continued)

	Now	Future
13. Our product and service is better than the competition's.	___	___
14. Product and service quality are measured routinely.	___	___
15. Quality and quality improvements are encouraged.	___	___
16. Productivity and productivity improvements are encouraged.	___	___
17. The organization encourages innovation.	___	___
18. The organization is aggressive, willing to take risks.	___	___
19. The organization has exciting new products in progress.	___	___
20. Management has focus. It knows where it is going.	___	___
21. Management responds when there is a problem.	___	___
22. Management anticipates. We plan ahead.	___	___
23. Management implements well.	___	___
24. Long-term profitability drives the organization.	___	___
25. Morale is good; the company has team spirit.	___	___
26. Compensation is fair and competitive.	___	___
27. Where appropriate, effective incentive compensation programs are in place.	___	___
28. Benefits are good.	___	___
29. Working conditions are pleasant.	___	___
30. There is good opportunity for personal growth and career development.	___	___
31. Employees are provided the tools and training to do their jobs.	___	___
32. Employees feel generally secure in their jobs.	___	___
33. We are ethical in our treatment of employees and customers.	___	___
34. The organization and its employees contribute to the community.	___	___

APPENDIX B

Action Plan Matrix (000)

Name of Action Plan	Person Resp.	First Year:					Second Year:					Third Year:				
		Gross Sales	Profit	Add'l Expn.	Cap. $ Needed	Add'l People Needed	Gross Sales	Profit	Add'l Expn.	Cap. $ Needed	Add'l People Needed	Gross Sales	Profit	Add'l Expn.	Cap. $ Needed	Add'l People Needed
TOTALS:																

NOTES

NOTES

NOTES

NOTES

NOTES

OVER 150 BOOKS AND 35 VIDEOS AVAILABLE IN THE 50-MINUTE SERIES

We hope you enjoyed this book. If so, we have good news for you. This title is part of the best-selling *50-MINUTE™ Series* of books. All *Series* books are similar in size and identical in price. Many are supported with training videos.

To order *50-MINUTE* Books and Videos or request a free catalog, contact your local distributor or Crisp Publications, Inc., 1200 Hamilton Court, Menlo Park, CA 94025. Our toll-free number is (800) 442-7477.

50-Minute Series Books and Videos Subject Areas . . .

Management
Training
Human Resources
Customer Service and Sales Training
Communications
Small Business and Financial Planning
Creativity
Personal Development
Wellness
Adult Literacy and Learning
Career, Retirement and Life Planning

Other titles available from Crisp Publications in these categories

Crisp Computer Series
The Crisp Small Business & Entrepreneurship Series
Quick Read Series
Management
Personal Development
Retirement Planning

DATE DUE

APR 16 '98			